v v v

A BEAUTIFUL DARKNESS

Second Edition

v v v

ROBERT JAI OWENS

v v v

ISBN: 979-8-3485-1671-0

Copyright 2024

This book is a work of fiction. Names, characters, places, and incidents either are products of the author's imagination or are used fictitiously. Any resemblance to actual events or locals or persons, living or dead, is entirely coincidental.

All rights reserved, including the right of reproduction in whole or in Part in any form.

About the Author

I was born and raised in the vibrant city of Los Angeles, where the creative energy of south-central LA shaped my early life. Growing up, I was deeply drawn to the art form of hip-hop music, which I saw as a fusion of poetry, music, and rhythm. As I delved deeper into the genre, I realized that hip-hop's core elements - the beats, the rhymes, and the storytelling - resonated deeply with my own passion for words and self-expression.

As a hip-hop enthusiast turned author, I'm excited to share my thoughts, feelings, and perspectives with the world. Although I know that not everyone will resonate with my words, I hope that my work will inspire, provoke, and connect with readers on a deep level. I know you can't please everyone but I hope you like it peace.

Contents

- About the Author ... 3

BOOK ONE ... 12
- Swimming Upstream ... 13

The Diddler ... 14

Tomorrow's Not Promised ... 15
- What Is It ... 16
- Delilah's Lesson ... 17
- A Journey Ends ... 18
- Vote ... 19
- Oasis ... 20

Money ... 21
- 3 At The Altar ... 22
- Inner City Memo ... 23
- Peace ... 24
- One And the Same ... 25
- Old Too Soon Smart Too Late ... 26
- The Sparkle B4 Dimming ... 27
- Winter Desires ... 28
- 1,2,3 ... 29
- I Want 2 Get Off ... 30
- Different but the Same ... 31
- Never Buy or Give ... 32
- Don't Let Your Dreams Slip Away ... 34

Fame	35
Time	36
Free Will	38
The Mighty Are Falling	39
Once You Treat Her Like a Star	40
Kiss	41
L.O.V.E	42
A Faint Calling	43
Destiny is a Fickle little Bitch	44
I Didn't Know How To Respond	46
Many Moons Ago	48
Ghetto Azz Grey's Anatomy	49
One Day	51
Love's Unwritten Rule	52
Legends Die Hard	53
Images and Information	55
No More Options	56
Imperfect Friend	58
Teenage PTSD in the Hood	59
The Goat	60
Madness	62
The Season Love Ends	63
Dandelions Wish	64
Krown Royal	65

MEG	66
K-Dot Vs Drizzy	67
2 is better than 1	68
Hypocritical Library	69
He Did It Again	71
Unafraid	72
Polar Bear Ice	74
Hip Hop s first Superstar	75
US	77
You'll Never See It Written	78
Cupid's biggest sin	79
Empaths Of Society	80
Stay Gold	81
Can I Ride With You	82
I've Seen the Light	84
In Another Life	85
Together	87
What Would I Say	88
I Don't Deserve You	90
I Know What It Means	91
Crystal Ball	92
The Beast Inside Me	93
If I fell 4U	94
Undeniably Beautiful	95

Each Dawn I Die 96

One Child's Story 97

L.O.S.T 98

Falling 99

One Direction 100

My Sentimental Heart Can't Lie Anymore 101

2Pacalypse Now and Forever 102

What Do You Want 104

The Pain of Living with Pockets of joy 105

Warrior's For Christ 106

It Happens Out of Nothing 109

Noose for a Youth 110

The Relationship from Hell 111

An Angels Love 113

.... 114

Concrete Jungle Raymond Ave 115

BOOK TWO 2

At The End of Your Play 3

Swan Song 4

Silly Azz Love Poem 5

Always Here 6

The Wind Blows 7

The Scale 8

Where Ever God Sends Her 9

- Integrity 10
- The Padawan & The Chosen one 11
- Break My Heart 13
- Cupid Can't Wait 14

The Combination 15

- Cupid's Blunder 18
- A Mother's Love 19
- Eazy -E 20

THE BURNING KINGDOM OF BRIMSTONE 22

- The Burning Kingdom of Brimstone Part 1 23
- The Burning Kingdom of Brimstone Part 2 24
- The Burning Kingdom of Brimstone Part 3 25
- The Burning Kingdom of Brimstone Part 4 26
- The Burning Kingdom of Brimstone Part 5 27
- The Burning Kingdom of Brimstone Part 6 28

SAD CLOWN 30

- Sad Clown Part 1 31
- Sad clown Part 2 32
- Sad Clown Part 3 33
- Sad Clown Part 4 34
- Sad Clown Part 5 35
- Sad Clown Part 6 36
- Sad Clown Part 7 37
- Sad Clown Part,8 38

Sad clown Part 9 39

Sad Clown Part 10 40

I Still Love You So 41

D.e.r.e.o.n 42

UFOs Or Drones 43

Cries & Lies 44

Key 2 Righteousness 45

Choose 46

kindness Is A Curse 47

Boss Lady 48

Bob Marley 50

A Hard Farewell 51

Childhood Missed 52

A Beautiful Darkness 53

Trip 2 Hell 54

Coming home from war 55

Damsel 56

Love Makes You Feel 57

Calm before the Storm 58

You Can Lose 59

Before 60

Life Can Still Amaze 61

Find What You are looking for 62

Paradise Lost 63

- Who Am I ... 64
- Learning 2 Flourish ... 65
- Eternity Begins ... 66
- The Fractured Lights ... 67
- Love's Only Value Exist ... 68
  - Let Me Down Easy ... 69
  - The Question Is? ... 70
  - The Juice is Free ... 71
  - Life Care ... 72
- Love Is Like Wine ... 73
  - You Have 2 Live with Yourself ... 75
  - Reciprocated ... 77
  - The Inevitable ... 78
  - Queen of Today & Tomorrow ... 79
  - You Left Me Too Soon ... 80
  - The Pursuit of Happiness ... 81
  - Down the Line ... 82
  - What is Loneliness ... 83
  - Marvelous Marvin Gaye ... 84
  - The Galveston Giant ... 85
  - Betrayal ... 86
- Cast Out For All 2 See ... 87
  - The End ... 88

BOOK ONE

Swimming Upstream

Miracles are what happens
When you put in the work
You can't keep a man down
With out sharing the dirt

We are what we are
From the very beginning
The losers want it all
Without the struggle of winning

Anything worth having
God made it hard
Blood diamonds in the hands of a child
Always looks scared

But once the chores are all done
And the jewels are polished
The lives of the slaves that made you rich
Are always demolished

With no 40 acres and a mule
Not even respect
But I guess a hanging noose
Is just right for a neck

Yet the times are always changing
And people always evolving
Why can't we all get along
So we can start resolving

Because wars cost money
Peace doesn't cost a thing
So why do we as human beings
Continue to swim upstream

The Diddler

A Roman orgy of sorts
that is fit for a King
The host plays between the legs of young ladies
Until they all start to sing

Trays are past around
Full of drugs and lube
So that he can more easily bend their will
And keep them in the mood

But unbeknown to the guest
The host has 3 eyes
The evil ones that he glares with
And his cameras that are disguised

As he stands butt naked at the party
Just like the statue of David
And tells all of his horny victims
That " I am so glad that you can make it "

To the party of the year
Where everyone will be hard, wet, high and soft
Until a 1000 bottles of baby oil are all gone
At the Diddlers annual freak off.

Tomorrow's Not Promised

I can hear the rain outside
While the sun lights up the sky
Is this truly tears of joy
When the Lord cries

Or is it merely just the norm
Just a magnificent sun shower
A beautiful display
Of mother nature's power

But I guess it doesn't matter
As I stand here and marvel
At the promise of today
That is not promised tomorrow.

What Is It

What is the one thing in your life
That barely keeps you afloat
Keeps your head above water
Just enough so you won't choke

Allows you to exist
But keeps you from truly living
Keeps the animal inside you caged
To prevent you from killing

Drain you of all your
time, energy and hope
So much until It's hard
For any decent human being to cope

And you will be programmed to perform
In all sorts of stormy weather
Because of the little piece of paper
That holds your life together

And when you're no longer needed
You will be replaced
And if you're not dead or too old
It begins again only in a new place

Plus the only option is
Too kill, steel, or rob
If you don't bow down
And be a slave to a job...

Delilah's Lesson

God has blessed you with strength
And also an Achilles heel
Keep that which makes you vulnerable to yourself
Or risk having your fate completely sealed

The fairer sex can entice and enchant
With their poisonous nectar and charms
But let us not forget the strongest man on this earth
Was destroyed by the woman that lay in his arms

A Journey Ends

Life is a journey
That starts with a single step
And will not reach fruition
Till there are no more steps left...

Vote

Echoing applause and cheers from supporters
As the presidential candidate speaks about the border
Shots ring out at an event that's surrounded by reporter's
Perhaps now we should discuss how we need law & order

Because there are too many guns
In the hands of the irritable
Who don't know how to disagree
Without being violently disagreeable

So the next time it feels like
A politician is cutting your throat
Assassination is not necessary
When all you have to do is vote

VOTE

Oasis

Some would rather be indulged
Rather than make a contribution
And continue to be Part of the problem
Instead of the solution

While some travel far and wide
To exploit this fair land not to embrace it
We should show more respect
And gratitude to the one place the world
Still calls an oasis

Money

When you look like money
People want you to spend it
And depending on who's in your pockets
It won't take but a minute

For you to lose everything
Down to your self-esteem
No more lovers or friends
With nothing in between

So keep it old school
Your money never flaunt it
Even if you're rich
You tell people you don't got it

Because the moment that you don't
Is when you need to worry
Because we're only viable
As long as we're necessary

And if we're no longer necessary
Then we're no longer viable
Keep this in mind with your money
Or lose it to undesirables.

MONEY

3 At The Altar

I'm trapped in a relationship
That is of my making but not of my wish
And if I don't marry
I'll find myself in a ditch

I got my girlfriend pregnant
We're both pretty young
And now It's us 3 at the altar
Me my girlfriend and her daddy's shotgun

Inner City Memo

We went from being brothers & sisters
2 being niggaz and bitches
But the finger pointing game is lame
And not da same

We need 2 all come together
One love and one people
And digress from the stereotypes
that make us look evil

Police our own hoods
No mercy for the wicked
We need the bravest and the smartest
Kingz & Queenz 2 fix this

4 every day is a gift
So recognize da blessing
That's why da here and the now
Is considered the present

So get up off yo AZZ
And help make a change
Because evolution & revolution
Goes hand and hand with pain

Thus open up your minds
Because it's time to learn
Or get left behind
Once da wheels of history have turned........

INNER CITY MEMO

Peace

Peace is what we all should strive for
Even if it means going to war
Angels will be at the gates of our demise
Cemetery plaques of name's with no disguise
Embrace peace on their backs with dead eyes & open skies

P.E.A.C.E

One And the Same

I wasn't very close to my dad
His past was full of pain
Losing his mom as a teen
I guess makes it hard to maintain

Almost dying for a country
That doesn't give a damn
What are the odds of being born
But yet, here I am

Broken like my father
But in a different way
Just trying to keep my sanity
Living day to day

My dad didn't leave me much
Just the blood that ran through his veins
And this paranoia that makes our pain
Now one and the same

Old Too Soon Smart Too Late

The only thing that ever mattered
Was already gone
Peace love and understanding
My family bond

Imploded then exploded
Into distant strangers
Living individual lives
Leaving our family's future endangered

With so many of us now
We act like a few
How did we ever come to this
I don't have a clue

By the time I realized
I couldn't change our fate
That's when I knew
That I was old too soon and smart too late

The Sparkle B4 Dimming

The sparkle and the dimming
So lovely in the beginning
Young, strong, & fast
addicted to only winning

Whatever is in the way
somehow becomes the way
When in pursuit of all of my dreams
please don't get in my way

Because I will annihilate
And swallow your soul
B4 the lights go dim
6 feet deep in a hole.

THE SPARKLE B4 DIMMING

Winter Desires

Freezing temperatures outside
Inside of a cabin, a cozy place
All alone with my heart's desire
Finally we're face to face

The only sound that we can hear
Is the crackling of the fireplace and the wind
Two rapidly beating hearts from anxiety
Right before the love making begins

We slowly embrace one another
With our truest feelings and no more lies
As she looks up at me with anticipation
And I look down into her eyes

Because I now realize exactly how
I want to experience eternity
Because to live without this woman's love
Would certainly be absurdity

So we lie down on the bear skinned rug
To consummate our love by the warmth of the fire
Away from the freezing cold that's outside
So we can fulfill our winter desires

WINTER DESIRES

1,2,3

In the time it takes to blink
Your life will flash before your eyes
Funny how past events
Can instantaneously fly

Right before the end
And your spirit is set free
You will see your whole life
Before you can count 1, 2, 3.

1, 2, 3

I Want 2 Get Off

7 days a week
12 months a year
Birthday after birthday
Cheers in your ear

A boy becomes a man
Glowing in his prime
Nothing is out of reach
He says, "Anything could be mine"

But years become decades
Players become played
Half a century has past
And Your youth starts to fad

then Your rock hard body
Becomes pathetically soft
That's when you say to yourself
Stop the calendar, I want 2 get off.

Different but the Same

Colorism is light skinned daughters
And dark skinned son's
A community of combatants
Where nobody won

Just Crabs in a barrel
Pulling each other down
With other nationalities in attendance
Just standing around

As they chuckle at the sight
Of the inhumanity
Of those Who don't see themselves in one another
The reverse of vanity

How did we ever come to this
Is Jim crow to blame
But even if it is
Why do we fan the flames

Until the black experience is now
More than we can bear
Where we have become spectacles in this society
And nobody cares....

Never Buy or Give

Never buy any woman
Flowers & candy
Never buy any woman
Top shelf Brandy

Never buy any woman
Diamonds and pearls
Because for absolutely nothing
Pookie F@#ks yo girl

Never give any woman
All of your time
Never give any woman
Your very last dime

Never let a woman
who stray's in her prime
Try a boomerang
When she's in her decline

And best believe what I say
Because what I say is true
Because without a dime or doing time
Ray Ray creams your Suzy Q

So you better be selective
Who you claim for a Princess or Queen
And keep in mind that

Just because these women shine
Doesn't mean that they gleam.

NEVER BUY OR GIVE.

PS
Not taking shots at the good women
Out there
Only the bad one's

Don't Let Your Dreams Slip Away

A Dream is just a dream
Until it becomes real
But what are we willing to do for this prize
When it's time to move in for the kill

Will we let it slip through our fingers
Like sand while we're standing on the beach
Or learn from others mistakes
When they unknowingly teach from defeat

So love and lose while you still can
And slow dance from night till day
But whatever you do my loved ones
Don't let your dreams slip away

Fame

For some people fame is forever
Even after all of the cheers
And the talent that you've displayed
That has been dormant for years

So say goodbye to the privacy
That you took for granted as an unknown
Because now and for the rest of your life
You will never be alone

To do the simplest of things
Like disappear into your thoughts
Only to be awaken by your fans
Saying that fame has a cost.

Fame

Time

Time is most precious
Time is currency
More valuable than gold
But unrealized until you're old

Time should be respected
Funny how we don't
We always tell ourselves that we will
But so many of us won't

Time is the only thing
That we can never get back
And it will continue to move on
Even when we fade to black

For once it passes by
It will never come back
And it will linger in our thoughts
Of a time when we were at

A better or worse place
That maybe left a bitter taste
But whatever it use to be
That time will never be replaced

And that breaks my heart
I wish time was my friend
How great and wonderful would it be
To go back and start again

And 2 maybe speed it up
Or maybe slow it down
It is what it is
Even at the speed of sound

I can still hear the rolling stones singing
Time is on my side
But now the truth has been revealed
And that song was a lie

Just ask anyone who's doing time
That is far far away
And they will tell you
That the punishment isn't being locked up
It's when they take your time away.

TIME

Free Will

What is free will
To act without constraints
Or maybe stand and deliver
On what one thinks

Perhaps move through the universe
At your own discretion
conceivably take someone else's life
In times of aggression

Perchance use your intellect
To feed off ignorance
While The poor and middle class
will believe that you're brilliant

But all I really know
Is that we really don't know
And free will when stripped down
Means that you can leap inside a volcano

Or it could just be that
Free will is deceptive
And if you think everyone shouldn't have it
Then you're very perceptive

FREE WILL

The Mighty Are Falling

Demigods and false idols
Along with people who sell their souls
The day of your reckoning is at hand
Now it's time to be exposed

And let the world see What lies beneath
All of the glitz & glamour
Before the long arm of the law
Comes down with a mighty hammer

And takes away every single thing
That makes you feel so important
The Grammy's, fame and dirty cash
Not to mention all of the coke that your snorting

But worry not privileged one's
For the illuminati has a plan
And it's gonna be a hard knock life 4U
When your high life starts to land.

Once You Treat Her Like a Star

Being in a relationship with some women
Is no different than celebrity and fame
Most seek and need validation
To continue their reign

But once you make the mistake
of treating her like a star
She will slowly but surely
Forget who you are

Nonetheless by then
You will cease to be her man
Because once you treat a woman like a starlet
She will treat you like a fan.

ONCE YOU TREAT HER LIKE A STAR

Kiss

Slow dancing with the devil
With my hands on her ass
As she whispers in my ear
"Make love like it's the last"

So I pulled her close to me
In the pale moon light
When all of a sudden
The sky abruptly ignites

I hold her in my grasp
And kiss her on her neck
As she moans in my ear
That "this will be a night
that you will never forget"

But forget I soon will
As she takes my last breath
With her soft lips and black eyes
I succumb to death

But I can still hear her voice saying
"That only now do you see
Every road you've ever traveled
Would return you to me"

"But fear me not lover
As I fill your heart full of bliss
Because even in the afterlife
We can still kiss"

KISS

L.O.V.E

Love has me drifting in outer space

Orbiting around hearts that can never be replaced

Voyaging into a realm where pain is love

Ending all of my bonds that were forged in blood

L.O.V.E

A Faint Calling

Stuck between two worlds
Reality and a beautiful unknown
The physical realm that I reside in
Is far from perfect but it's still home

But the unknown has this golden glow
And this feeling of undeniable peace
In one ear I can hear a faint whisper
And the other many crying and a priest

And now I feel indecisive because I now realize
The in-between is my spirit falling
But what are you supposed to do
When you realize those whispers are the Angels calling...

Destiny is a Fickle little Bitch

Destiny is without a doubt
A fickle little bitch
I thought that all of my future plans
Would go off without a hitch

Love and happiness
Living in paradise
Has been reduced to eating meals
With no meat with my rice

Blasphemous rumors in my life
echo every single day
That I would never be able to shape my future plans
and sculpt them like clay

With a beautiful wife, kids, home
and a dog
On a quiet country side
like a Shakespear 's eclogue

But destiny is no more
And fades away as the sunsets
I look toward the sky
and ask the Lord am I done yet

There was no reply
Just some old guy digging a ditch

He looked up at me from the hole he was digging
And said that "Destiny is a fickle little bitch"

I Didn't Know How To Respond

Because we don't know How to respond
Usually We don't respond
Other people problems
Are always a step beyond

If I intervene and come in-between
A beautiful wife & handsome groom
That's headed to there doom
How do you tell newlyweds to give each other room

Domestic battles turns into wars
That love can't endure
And the children of holy matrimony
Becomes casualties of that war

Now we have kids
In a one parent home
With an overbearing mother
Or a dad that is always gone

The male child joins a gang
The young girl turns to prostitution
Because of an unmitigated situation
That has absolutely no solutions

Now the family is forever broken
No matter how much the grandmother prays
And all I can do is look
With my eyes in a glazes

If I had only spoken up
And prevented this tragedy
Of two different worlds
Colliding personalities

So I turn my back against the wind
And start to walk on
Because I didn't know how to respond
So I didn't respond.

I DIDN'T KNOW HOW TO RESPOND

Many Moons Ago

Many moons ago
there was a glow
That radiated like the sun
Since time had begun

Elusive yet it's still there
Very uncanny
We'll never understand our purpose
in this God forsaken life are can we

Many moons ago
The hourglass of time
Was created to remind us
That not everything ages like wine

Something's break down
And get very decrepit
The sands of time are so unforgiving
That we can never reset it

For time is always moving
That's why the hourglass is cracked
So we will always keep in mind
That we can never go back

Many moons ago
In my youth time was forever
But now that radiating glow of life
Has been completely severed.

MANY MOONS AGO.

Ghetto Azz Grey's Anatomy

When I go to work
I shake hands with the dying
I interact with people that are always lying
My work is back breaking
There ain't no denying
If you get too attached
You might start crying
My work is serious
But not that serious
For nosy MF
To be so damn curious
How much money do you make
Who do you be F@#kin
You'll never hear a thing out of me
So you're shit out of luckin
So walk away in your scrubs
And go show your patients Some love
In this ghetto azz Grey's Anatomy
No members having azz club
Because when I receive my paycheck
I know I'm being paid to stay in check
But if I ever go postal in my scrubs
Somebody better hit the deck
Because I've had it up to here
I'm talking year after year
I should be somewhere drunk
Like a f#@king episode of cheers
Or maybe laughing and smiling
Like I'm watching a sitcom

Instead I go to work
And it's like I'm back in Vietnam
Well maybe not back
That was before my time
But still you get the picture
That's why I'm going out of my mind
Since all I smell is shit
And work with kids that still pop zits
This ghetto azz Grey's Anatomy
Has got me having a fit
That's why I stay f@#ked up
Off a bottle of Remy
The only thing my job is missing
Is that B list actor Patrick Dempsey
So he can diagnose me
At this ghetto azz Grey's Anatomy
And prescribe me a one-way trip
Right off of this f@#king balcony.

GHETTO AZZ GREY'S ANATOMY

One Day

Why do I still care
After so many terrible things
Once you were my fantasy
More beautiful than anything I've ever seen

But the warmth of the sun is fading
Rapidly as the seasons change
The dead of winter will numb my bleeding heart
So that I may one day love again

ONE DAY

Love's Unwritten Rule

Why is it so hard
To love the one you're with
You both keep your silence about love
But in the back of your mind you are saying this is it

So you play the game of love
By seeing how disrespectful you can get
Or how much disrespect the other will allow
Before someone gets hit

But the unwritten rule of a love that is true
Was forged and created with fire
And when it finally cooled and was ready to read
It said never hurt that which you desire

Legends Die Hard

Legends die hard
Underneath the stars
Remember James Dean
And how he died in his car

Remember JFK
My favorite Playboy president
Who was assassinated in 63
And possibly by his own f@#king government

He said "we don't do things because they are easy
We do them because they are hard"
And on July of 1969
The moon was f@#king ours

And we all remember John Lennon
All you need is love
But one night in 1980
He was gone from 38 slugs

Legends die hard
Just ask Marilyn Monroe
She had sex with JFK and his brother
And was labeled a hoe

God don't like ugly
But history has shown
That the biggest sinners in the world
Are the ones who throw stones

We also lost Michael Jackson
The king of pop
Who sang and danced like no other
Until his heart stopped

We can also look back with love
To Martin Luther King and I have a dream
That turned into a nightmare
As Americans scream

Love is gonna get' cha
But not before violence get' cha
And you leave this world as martyr
And paint a perfect picture

Legends die hard
Like the late Malcolm X
Who tried to bring change
And died like the next

Just remember in the end
To all you women and men
That Jesus died on the cross
So that you could live again.

LEGENDS DIE HARD.

Images and Information

Be careful of images and information
We allow ourselves to receive
For once it is there
It will be hard for it to leave

Images of crime, violence, and sex
Coupled with Disloyalty, greed and a God complex
Will put our morals in a blender
And love letters returned to sender

But if they took the time to read it
It would have said surrendered
Yet the price of burning bridges
Is that they always seem to remember

So please be mindful of toxic information
And the things that we read
Because the slightest tap can move us
To a lonely place, in our hour of need.

IMAGES and INFORMATION...

No More Options

Too be so young
vibrant and free
And to have men of all ages
Down on their knees

To pay homage at the feet
Of a dazzling Goddess
Women like this
Have never been modest

Perfect in every way
Imperfections she'll crush
For just a batting of her eyes
Is enough to make God's blush

With her high hill stilettos
She can easily walk on water
Self-made in every way
Except for the things that men have bought her

And so the years fly by
With no gratitude just attitude
Flying high in this life
Like she'll never lose altitude

And run the same game
That involves worship & rejection
With men lined up
Willing to do anything for their erection

Or perhaps risk it all
For a flower that is so lovely
But even the most beautiful of flowers
Will one day grow to be ugly

And now all of the young men
That stopped to smell the roses
Are now older and successful
And now turn up their noses

To yesterday's news
A Goddess that was so rotten
Has had one to many birthdays
And has now run out of options.

NO MORE OPTIONS

Imperfect Friend

More than anyone that I can think of
You were my truest friend
We didn't always get along
But you were always there till the end

We had a lot of memories
Some of them were even good
But I wouldn't change a thing
Even if I could

Life is so unpredictable
I guess we're all born to lose
And destined to shed tears
When we get the bad news

That a loved one or friend
Who battled with so many demons within
Has left us all behind
Too some place better than they've been.

Teenage PTSD in the Hood

The older that I get
I realize that my life was f@#ked
Surviving neighborhood gangs
On just mere luck

The 80's was a monster
The 90's was a curse
How many adolescents do you know
That day dream about riding in a Hurst

I remember bullets flying
And single black mother's crying
Because their teenage sons
Are being shot down and dying

From crooked ass cops
That have the mark of the beast
That won't hesitate to power trip
And knock out your teeth

Or drop you off Across town
In an enemy's neighborhood
Where you might not make it back
If you're a Crip being dropped off in Inglewood

With low riders everywhere
As far as I can see
While I try and survive the hike back
With this PTSD

So I continue on my mission
And do what I got to do
Because these boyz in the hood are some killers
But I'm a killer too.

TEENAGE PTSD IN THE HOOD

The Goat

You were like a god on this earth
when you were in your prime
In your Kentucky fried voice
You said the world is mine

Your star would shine brighter
Than a billion suns
Fighting monsters in the ring
And made it look fun

You always made time
For the poor and the weak
And kept your head held high
When our leaders were put 2 sleep

You were a Tyrannosaurus Rex
With a beautiful face
And always stood your ground
When confronted with hate

But father times hourglass
Runs out for us all
Who ever would have thought
That the Greatest would fall
I know your enemies cheered
When your health declined
But God is all love
And I know that you're fine

In a garden of pleasure
Jannah paradise
Standing in the light
Of eternal life

And I hope this poem finds your ears
With much peace and love
And puts a smile on your face
As you watch from above

So Assalamu Aalaikum champ
You're Deserving of a shrine
May God bless your soul
The greatest of all time.

Dedicated to my hero Muhammad Ali the greatest of all time.

Madness

I wish there was someone that I can talk 2
Someone 2 convey my deepest thoughts
A single soul that would follow my voice
Without the fear of getting lost

In the darkness and the shame
Of he who remains
Who has come to the end of God's gift
With nothing else to gain

So please continue to follow my voice
The one with undertones of sadness
Till you put your ear next to my breathless lips
And I whisper and explain why life is madness.

The Season Love Ends

I guess here's the season
To intertwine with treason
But then again traders
Never really need a reason

To kill relationships
And murder friendships
But what else could it be
When there's no more courtships

Because love is a relic
If I let you tell it
That once upon a time
Was as smooth as velvet

But ladies are no more
And gentlemen are no more
Reduced to the very thing
That past generations deplore

But now that chivalry Is dead
And honor is put to bed
"With this ring I thee wed"
So I can live in dread

But Unbeknown is the season
That my love will end
When I already know
That it ends when it begins.

Dandelions Wish

On no particular day
I see Dandelions in the hands of a child
She was Wearing tattered clothes, uncombed hair
And had a painful smile

I watched her close her eyes
As she makes a wish
With tears rolling down her face
On to her busted lip

Then the child puckered up in pain
And blew the dandelions into the wind
Whispering to God, let this be when and where my new life begins

All I could do is just sigh
For I am just a stranger who is passing through
As I watched the dandelions passing by
I also made a wish too

And my only wish is for the child to be saved
From a life that is so blue
And for all of the young girl's wishes
To finally come true.

DANDELIONS WISH.

Krown Royal

Knowledge is infinite
Rules that make you clever
Oasis is the basics of love that stays together
War is necessary to maintain the peace
Never compromise your values or beliefs

Reckless in your thoughts reflects in your behavior
Only god can judge me, so no one is above me
You have to love yourself before anybody else
Ask and you shall receive all of your wealth
Last but not least remember life is a test
do what works 4u and f@#k the rest.

KROWN ROYAL.

MEG

You were my first crush
When I was 15
You were 28
A Goddess and a Queen

With your jet-black hair
And exquisite beauty
So exotic and erotic
Together we'd be melodic

In an imperfect world
With the perfect intentions
Meg Tilly you're the charm
That this prince has been missing

So all hail the Queen
The girl in a swing
Who still captivates me
Even as KING.

Dedicated to Margaret Elizabeth Chan A.K.A
Meg Tilly

K-Dot Vs Drizzy

Clash of the titans
K-dot VS Drizzy
We're about to turn up
And get lyrically busy

Canada VS the US
2 be the undisputed King
As they step into the booth
And commence to hip hop sing

I don't know who will win
All I know is that the fans will feel your presence
And thank you for returning hip hop
2 its battle field essence

From Taylor made to push ups
To Euphoria and 6:16 in LA
This has been the battle of the ages
With monumental air play

So may the best man win
And emerge victorious
With out repeating the mistakes
Of 2Pac and Notorious

K-DOT VS DRIZZY

2 is better than 1

Mother's day should be everyday

And Father's Day should not be forgotten

Because the fruit that doesn't fall far from the tree

Needs both parents 2 not prematurely grow up 2 be rotten

2 IS BETTER THAN 1

Hypocritical Library

The simplicity of dying
And the difficulty of living
From day one when we enter this world
Nothing is given

From the root to the fruit
Till the day that we mute
The meek of the earth shall
Inherit a boot

And at the end of that boot
Is a colonial tyrant
Who's single goal objective
Is to keep you silent

And take what they want
Keep you a pawn
Blind you to a struggle
That prevents you from
Seeing beyond

Into your own life's purpose
Instead of being in service
To a selfish tyrant
That makes you feel worthless

It's time for us to be notorious
And to feel vainglorious
Or die with simplicity
Because our life's laborious

So when you think of liberty
And the powers that be
Ask yourself if that same
Library applies to me.

HYPOCRITICAL LIBRARY

He Did It Again

The greatest come back
In political history
Some in a state of shock
Like this is a mystery

But love him or hate him
He won 4 more years
To lead a divided nation
Full of boos and cheers

HE DID IT AGAIN.

Unafraid

The doctors diagnosed me yesterday
With something detrimental
That really had me shook
And messed with my mental

I could no longer sleep
My future was in peril
Time is no longer on my side
Tomorrow is getting narrow

Every single day now
My heart is beating out of my chest
Thinking about my demise
And how can I pass this test

So I fall to my knees
And asked God, What can I do
To get through such a terrible thing
That everybody goes through

There was no response
But I know God is always there
To fight the battles that I can't
When war is declared

And then out of nowhere
Instead of thoughts of the grave
God finally blessed me
With not being afraid

He took away my fear
And showed me the beauty of life
Is ultimately coming to the end
So you can be with Christ

Now I understand
And thankful for the life that I made
And thankful for God's blessing
Of finally being unafraid.

UNAFRAID.

Polar Bear Ice

When I finally found out
That life isn't fair
That's when I became cold as the ice
Under a polar bear

Screaming at the top of my lungs
"Is anybody there"
Because I know there's someone else
Who knows my despair

And why my eyes tear up
Just to burn for no reason
Every time I look into the mirror
And see a f@#king heathen

That's why I hate my reflection
And I've learned not to care
Once I found out that I was cold as the ice
Under a polar bear.

POLAR BEAR ICE

Hip Hop s first Superstar

The first rapper to breath fire
And leave other rappers smoked
The one who doesn't get the love he deserves
But coined the phrase goat

Been in this game
Since the age of 16
A microphone fiend
Coming straight from Queens

Who took off like a rocket
When he said " I need love "
A pioneer from the beginning
Before he knew he was

10 times platinum
10 times in a row
Hold on 2 your seats
And enjoy the show

Radio, BAD, Walking with a panther
If there was ever any question
James Todd Smith
Was the answer

He has such a love for the culture
Hip hop was elevated
A rap icon
That should be celebrated

By climbing to the top of Mount Sion
From the bottom of hell
Too reach the peaks of his glory
Just to stand tall and rock the bells

Raps first superstar
Who refused to fail
And now without further ado
In the words of LL

" I'm a lyrical flame
On the heels of fame
And the world was glad
That Cool J came".

US

I see you
You see me
Soon the world will see we
Together as US.

You'll Never See It Written

There's a war being waged
On the landscapes of my mind
And doing the right things
Doesn't win all of the time

So let he or she without sin
Cast the first stone
But no stones will be thrown
Even if we all atone

For to live without sin
Is the great unknown
That is why you'll never See it written
On anybody's headstone

YOU'LL NEVER SEE IT WRITTEN

Cupid's biggest sin

Slowly burning this relationship
That was love at first sight
Oblivious to what is or what is not
With the wind howling through the night

Blind to what I need
and blind to what I want
Undoubtedly when love leaves
It leaves just to taunt

But I've said it before
And I'll say it again
To play with the emotions of someone's heart
Is Cupid's biggest sin.

CUPID'S BIGGEST SIN

Empaths Of Society

Empaths that exist
In this heartless world
Absorbing the unworthy feelings
Of use to be little boys and girls

Stop before the heart break
Becomes too much
Having empathy for anyone
That you so much as touch

Turn your head to the left
And just look away
Or turn your head to the right
And refuse to stay

Because I use to be just like you
Absorbing all the pain
Of the people who have hurt me
Till I went insane

And once you realize
Exactly what people are
How bizarre and how scared
No matter who they are

Because once it all computes
And downloads in your brain
You'll never see another
Human being the same again

So beware of psychopaths
And also sociopaths
Because you won't stand
A chance if you're an empath.

EMPATHS OF SOCIETY

Stay Gold

When you show someone
Mercy or any kind of meekness
Your always looked upon
with some kind of weakness

So in days of future past
Develop some kind of heartlessness
And put to bed and leave dead
What remains of your tolerance

As most can care less
if you live or if you die
And will take your independence
on the 4th of July

And will strip you of your
Dignity, self-esteem and wealth
Corrupt your core values
And sink your health

So if you want to stay gold
You must become bold
Or forever be changed
Once your warm heart turns cold

STAY GOLD.

Can I Ride With You

Can I ride with you
You're my dream come true
Many years have Passed by
But the passing is through

Now were living in the moment
Joined at the hip
Two becomes one
When it's hers and his

So let no man or woman
Come in-between
Of this bound this union
This king this Queen

Or the unthinkable will happen
Light becomes dark
The eclipsing of your life
If you break my heart

We're at the point of no return
As our love transcends
To where it's longer to go back to the beginning
then it is to continue to the end

Because love is complicated
And life is complicated and when we're
Drunk off each other's love
We become intoxicated

Like Anthony and Cleopatra
John and Yoko
Sonny and char
So please be aware

That I want to make love 2U
Till the sun burns out
Hold you in my arms
Until the Oceans drought

Live every second
With no more sorrow
Money ain't a thang
As long as we die by tomorrow

But the dream will come no closer
We have to do more than just stare
The way I feel when I'm with you
Nothing can compare

That's why when I came into your life
And asked could I ride with you
It was simply because I knew
That you were my dream come true.

CAN I RIDE WITH YOU

I've Seen the Light

I was lost in the dark
Until I seen the light
At the top of Lone Mountain
This would be an impossible hike

With a busted leg
Freezing weather and an ugly ass sweater
But if I made it to the top
I knew I'd feel better

If I could just make it to this light
That's constantly calling me
It would be the answer to my prayers
I just know that it's got to be

So as I get closer and closer
To this blinding light
That's making it harder and harder to see
And affecting my sight

But soon I see a face
And it's my girl Corine
With her blond hair everywhere
And a devilish grin

Saying aren't you glad I flagged you down
Didn't you see the light
I just wanted to let you know
That everything is going to be alright

That's when my mouth dropped
I can't believe her
All that hiking for a f@#king flashlight
I wanted to kill her

Girl you're crazy
I don't know what to say
Next time I think God is showing me the light
I'm going the other way.

I SEEN THE LIGHT.

In Another Life

In another life
I would have been alright
Surrounded by love
Because I made a right

Instead I made a left
And met the angel of death
He whispered in my ears
About my dying last breath

That my life would be hard
Forever in harm
And that I'd never find a love
To hold in my arms

Yet even as I speak
To everything that sows & reaps
My hell is the abyss
That's eternally deep

So I will never stop falling
Through space and time
Grand & Noble in my thoughts
So I feel sublime

But in another life
I would have had a wife
From my earliest years
Till the end of my fears

But that will never happen now
Because I chose left instead of right
And so I'll walk on hot coals
For the rest of my life

But I often stop and think about
How my universe would have been so different
With all the blessings from above
Unlike my descendants

Even so you'll have to know
That in another life
In order for me to get it right
I'd have to live twice

So says the wheel of fortune
Every time it spends
The odds will always be against me
To where I can't win

But I bet no friends or even family
Will be willing to sacrifice
To walk a mile in my shoes
In this or any life.

IN ANOTHER LIFE.

Together

Together in prayer
Together in Christ
Together in love
Together in life
Together we fall
Together we fight
Together every day
Together every night
Together when it's good
Together when it's bad
Together when we're happy
Together when we're sad
Together on March 19th the first day of spring
Together when the bad weather produced our first fling
Together when I told you that I'm gonna love you better
Together when you told me that we're both two birds of a feather
Together when I said I can't live without you
And if I should die tonight
You said that we could do that too
TOGETHER.

What Would I Say

If I were to meet God
What would I say
Would I ask to live forever
And crave a love that just won't stay

Would I ask for rose petals
To fall at my feet
Every time I take a step
To let me know I'm unique

Or would I ask to change my past
And all of the things that traumatized me as a child
Plus give me the power to exact revenge
So I could eternally smile

Or maybe have my time back
To raise all of my babies
If I could sit down with the Almighty
I wonder what would he say to me

I guess that's why I'm scared
And lately I've begun to pray
Because in the event of my demise
If I'm judged by my deeds today

What would I say to the creator of all
Who is present everywhere at all times
In the physical & spiritual
And also the mind

Because he alone is eternal
And has always existed
He is completely self-sufficient
and independent
Of anything else in existence

So what would I say
Am I even worthy to speak
I guess I'll never know
Until I lay me down to sleep.

WHAT WOULD I SAY?

I Don't Deserve You

I can't be with you
Because I don't deserve you
The darkness I carry with me
Will one day come to hurt you

I've tried relentlessly
To wash my hands clean
But the deeds of my past
Even if unseen

Will eventually come around
And strike one of us down
Karma will show it's ugly face
And not make a sound

That's why I have to go away
Far away, so stay away
Don't try and talk me out of this
Because I just won't stay

And I'm not being selfish
This is what's best
You're everything I care for
But my feelings I must suppress

Now I must bid you goodbye
And for your best interest I must desert you
Notwithstanding the truth of the matter is
I just don't deserve you

So please don't hate me
More than I already hate myself
For You will always be my one true love
And after you there will never be anyone else.

I DON'T DESERVE YOU.

I Know What It Means

I was told that you'll never know love
Until your happiness is blown to smithereens
So I said to myself
"what the hell does that mean" ?

Then I thought about my ex
And how grotesque the murder scene
And then it finally dawned on me
I know what it means.

(((((((I KNOW WHAT IT MEANS)))))))

Crystal Ball

When I'm with you
I'm not thinking of anyone else
But if I'm with someone else
I'm always thinking of you

Could this be love
Or is it something else
I just know the Sun is always missing
When I'm by myself

So should I take a leap of faith
Beneath the wings of doves
Or come to the realization
That I will always be unlucky with love

Because God only knows
But the devil has shown
Through a Gypsy fortune tellers crystal ball
That I will always be alone.

CRYSTAL BALL.

The Beast Inside Me

Lord have mercy
I have this beast inside of me
That's wants to break free
From the bullshit rules of this society

Not only man's laws
But the 10 commandments
Means nothing anymore
Because of the circumstances

But What can I do
This beast wants to be free
And won't stop until my foes
Are 6 feet deep

Angels will try and come near
But I can see there aura
Through the trash and the Filth
Of Sodom and Gomorrah

I am not without sin
but I repent my ways
And anything in my way
The beast inside slays

I hope the Lord can forgive me
And understand how I feel
But how could this be wrong
When I just want to do God's will.

THE BEAST INSIDE ME

If I fell 4U

If I fell 4U
I'd never stop falling
Eternally silenced
And never stop calling

Find my way back 2U
No matter how far away
Forever came the day
That you decide to stay

But love is like life
The way it comes and goes
Beautiful when it comes
Painful when it goes

But make no mistake
About what cupid wants to do
With 2 lonely hearts
If I fell 4U.

Undeniably Beautiful

Undeniably beautiful & sexy
In every way
Parting ways with you is so hard
because I always want you to stay

Your eyes attracted me first
Because they made me smile with my heart
I never dreamed that a perfect woman could exist
But I knew it was you from the start

From your beautiful soft lips
And angelic smile
That makes me feel butterflies
I haven't felt in a while

So here's a toast to us
2 souls with 1 intention
As we sail into AMAR
To realize this lovely vision

Each Dawn I Die

My biggest regret
Is not being there for you
And not doing all of the things
That dads are my supposed to do

But don't misconstrue
Because each dawn, I die
And in my moments of solitude
I can't help but cry

But life is still good
Full of hidden lessons
And if you can't find forgiveness
Then I've learned my lesson

And if we can't reconcile
I'll understand why
I just needed you to know
That each dawn, I die.

Dedicated to Catherine A. Owens
[~I]
[~IX]

One Child's Story

Drowning in my pain
In rain that never stops
Visions of yesterday
Consuming all of my thoughts

My paradise was lost
I wish I could laugh
But childhood misery
Is all I seem to have

My hope is no more
My dreams 4 ever crushed
True love has been replaced
With meaningless lust

I pray that I can change
Or change what's around me
And live long enough
To say that GOD has found me

And stand in the sunlight
Of the supreme glory
And finally find redemption
2 one child's story

ONE CHILDS STORY

L.O.S.T

Lost in the moment
Lost in time
Lost in a dream of things to be mine
Lost in this world of impending danger

Where friends to the end become distant strangers
Lost in your eyes
Lost in love
Lost in the memories of everything that was

Lost in my thoughts
Lost in my illness
Lost in revenge and wishing I could kill this
Lost in religion

Lost in hope
Lost in drugs and praying that I can cope
Lost in lies
Lost in cries

Word 2 the wise everybody dies
Lost in greed
Lost in sex
Lost in the mist of what comes next.

LOST.

Falling

Standing with my back 2 a Cliff
I feel the warmth of the sun
I slowly lean backwards
Until my descent has begun

I'm falling so fast
With no bottom in sight
It's 2 late for me to turn back
Or even take flight

The only thing that I can do
Is feel the wind on my face
But I've been falling my whole life
So this is not a new place

The only thing that can save me now
Is if I suddenly faint
And my spirit leaves my body
Before it's too late

So Lord please forgive me
And save me a room
As I fall for the last time
Into my DOOM......

One Direction

One direction takes you days
The other direction takes you years

One direction leads to joy
The other direction leads to tears

One direction leads to life
The other direction leads to death

One direction gives you everything
The other direction there's nothing left

One direction has all the answers
The other direction knows life's a test

One direction is going nowhere
The other direction is on a quest.

My Sentimental Heart Can't Lie Anymore

Someone please tell me
Does hurt come from our truest words
Or would you love me more now
because of the lies that you've heard

It's hard to be me
or the person you are
Especially when we're nothing
but emotional scars

That was built from the trauma
of neglect and wreck
And all the heartache
that you'll never forget

Always told to get out
and sent to a sunken place
also filled with the kind of pain
That makes you put your hands in your face

Distressed at best
and friends with joylessness
Every day I feel the need
for a S.O.S

Because agony & misery
Has me in a state of emergency
And keeping a sane mind
is now a difficulty

So sorry for the way
that I express my woes
But my sentimental heart
can't lie anymore.

2Pacalypse Now and Forever

I can still hear your voice
The pain & the sorrow
Screaming thug life
Like there's no tomorrow

I see death around the corner
& If I die tonight
Self-proclaimed prophecies of
young black souls at night

Your image will never fade
Cradle to the grave
Imposters now try to walk
The Thug road you've paved

But they know nothing about struggle
Hunted by your trouble
and 25 years of being
trapped in a bubble

Until it finally burst
The gift & the curse
I shed so many tears
When you were laid in that hearse

But you will never be forgotten
No more tears for fears
For thug life will live on for a thousand years

So how long will we mourn
the late great one
Who taught us 2 persevere
Until the war is won

This is the story of a Soldier
That would never surrender
Who always spoke from his heart
And gave us something to remember.

Dedicated to my favorite rapper Tupac Amaru Shakur

What Do You Want

Why do you say you're ok
when you're really not
The truth of the matter is
You don't know what you want

But what you might want to know
Is that fame is not the goal
Money is not the goal
Because wealth without health
Soon takes its toll

And in your mind's eye
you will soon see
that all the best things
in this life are free

I'm talking money, cars, and gold
and even Yachts
Is insignificant to good health, true love
friends And wants

that will bring you
One step Closer to paradise
With your dreams In your hands
Now wouldn't it be nice

To have what you want
peace & love indeed
And still keep your soul
In your hour of need.

The Pain of Living with Pockets of joy

The pain of living
With pockets of joy
My Dad turned to my Mom
And said that it's a boy

My Dad held me high
Like the Dad in roots
And whispered into God's ears
Nothing but truth

In a poverty paradise
Of ghetto black life
My parents did their best I guess
To raise me right

But sometimes things change
Sometimes people change
And then the course that you were on
Will never be the same

And then love disappears
Like a thief in the night
From the ones you loved most
And have known all your life

And when you grow up to fast
Your loving heart turns cold
Because now you hold the reins
Of the life that you owe

So now mistakes will be made
From behaviors displayed
Like ignorant role models
With one foot in the grave

That's why the pain of living
With pockets of joy
Has been what it is
Since my Dad said that it's a boy.

THE PAIN OF LIVING WITH POCKETS OF JOY

Warrior's For Christ

Warriors for Christ
Is my new vice
Criminals of the night
You better Think twice

Because the son of our Father
Has ordained me
And if I punish you for your Sins
Then please don't blame me

Because you will hear Trumpet's
When it's time for justice
And you will see my weapon
When it's time to bust this

Lord have mercy
Why do I love this so
When evil bites the dust
No fuse it's only lust

For doing what I do
In the name of the Lord
Tearing through your flesh
With a flaming sword

No one will be spared
War has been declared
On all of God's children
So demons beware

When I'm on my world tour
Slaying Pimps and whores
And drug dealing scum
That prey on our young

Oh how I wish I Was there
When Jesus Was crucified
Because every last one of those
Roman's would die

And since I would be drunk
Drunk off revenge
And make no mistake
Your knees will Bend

With your hands behind your back
Head in a guillotine
I put this on Everything holy
This will be a gruesome murder Scene

With me dressed in all black
Like Keanu Reeves
but this will be nothing
like the days of Constantine

This will be the end
Of everyone with a vile life
And it will be by the hands of
Warrior's for Christ

So you better recognize
And get baptized

Cause when the holy war is On
You can't back slide

The only thing that you can do
Is ride for the cause
And be a warrior for Christ
Against all odds

I know the all mighty said that
"Vengeance is mine"
But the warrior in me
Says that it mines this time.

WARRIOR FOR CHRIST

It Happens Out of Nothing

It happens out of nothing
The fussing & cussing
Temper's get flared
Then here's comes the busting

In a New York minute
You don't have to be in it
But victims on the side lines
are seldom in it

Bad energy collides
Around innocent lives
And in the blink of an eye
The virtuous dies

It happens out of nothing
When trouble appears
But sometimes you can feel it
in the atmosphere

Your skin starts to crawl
At night in the fog
Anxiety is high
So you start to jog

But there's nowhere you can run
And nowhere you can hide
When it happens out of nothing
Your fate won't be denied.

IT HAPPENS OUT OF NOTHING.

Noose for a Youth

God has cursed me too see
What life should be like
When I was 12 years old
All I wanted was a bike

And have all the cool things
like the kids across town
I was a depressed adolescent
That was always down

child abuse was abundant
So I thought it was normal
In many ways it explains
How I grew to be humble

It was a hard knock life
With parents that were cold as ice
With no guidance or advice
I became a sacrifice

Waking up every day
Was like rolling the dice
But suicidal thoughts
Would also suffice

Oh what can I do
To remedy the insanity
I was always told that I was ugly
So there will never be vanity

In a skinny, tall awkward kid
Who's future is hopeless
And would have died at 13
If I knew where the rope was……

NOOSE FOR A YOUTH

The Relationship from Hell

The relationship from hell
Can't believe how far I fell
Holding on so long
Just waiting to exhale

Love can be cruel
A game without rules
But I guess everybody's
Somebody's fool

As far as I can see
I see nothing but ruins
A scorched earth love affair
From not knowing what I was doing

I've been to jail, cheated on
Miss used and disrespected
You told me who you are from day one
But I guess I still expected

A little bit more
A woman I could adore
Your body I would explore
Until I start to roar

But little did I know that your heart
Was full of malice
The pure definition
Of a woman who's callous

But there will soon come a day
When your deceit and treachery
Will come full circle
Like the days of you testing me

And then you'll soon know
That you reap what you sow
When your relationship s from hell
Are a one woman show

And when you're poor, broke, and lonely
In the depths you dwell
You will soon be reminded
Of how far I fell

In this relationship from hell
It ain't hard to tell
That at the end of your black rainbows
You won't be doing well

As I wonder What did I
Ever see in you
We would have never left the ground
If I only knew

So please brace yourself
4 instant karma
I hope you get devoured
By a school of piranhas

And that the skies open up

Just to strike you with lightning

So that your peace of mind be replaced

With dreams that are frightening.

And I pray every day
4 your dreams 2 come true
This was the relationship from hell
Dedicated 2U.

An Angels Love

Most impressive indeed
I'm surrounded by this glow
An angel held me in her wings
And wouldn't let me go

She said I've watched you through the clouds
Of rain dropped tears
And that even when you're whispering
Your voice echoes in my ears

Until I had to leave Valhalla
Seventh heaven and the rapture
With the beating of your heart
My love you have captured

And so I come to you beloved
To save you from oneself
Because we can never be
If you selfishly kill yourself.

Concrete Jungle Raymond Ave

My neighborhood was a jungle
But I had to survive
Ole English on my breath
With blood shot eyes

Every corner was infested
With kids from broken homes
On the hunt for fresh prey
If you dared to Walk alone

Getting chased by stray dogs
That foamed at the mouth
Hitting fences jumping benches
And running through a stranger's house

Ducking bullets after dark
At Hellen Keller Park
And fighting every day
Just to Prove I got heart

This is no way to live
But it's all that I got
South central LA
Winter times are hot

Because I live on Raymond Ave
Strapped up ready to blast
2 make it one more day
I got to give it all that I have

Or else I'll be dead
In a pool of red
While these animals
Pull me a Part just like warm bread

That's why I have to stay
Resilient, courageous & a Fox
Because one false move
Will put my ass in a box

My neighborhood ain't perfect
I'm sure you already know
But growing up in the hood
Is all I really know

That's why I never hold my breath
Expecting to laugh
In this concrete jungle
Known as Raymond Ave.

BOOK TWO

At The End of Your Play

Everyone's born to perform
And the world is our stage
Perfecting who we are
As we all come of age

But sooner or later
Time brings change
And the longer that we live
Our views on life won't be the same

Because we all feel pain
And we all have a past
Dreams that we would like to live
Before we inhale and exhale for the last

So don't put off for tomorrow
What you can do today
Remember who you are
The star of your own play

So enjoy this life to the fullest
Take a bow and enjoy the thunderous sound
Of the applause at the end of your life
Right before the curtain comes tumbling down.

AT THE END OF YOUR PLAY

Swan Song

When I look into your eyes
I can see the sadness
As I look a little deeper
I can see the madness

I can feel your sanity
Slowly slipping away
Fighting so hard
To keep the demons at bay

When I read your manuscripts
Beautiful dark tells
Of a woman who's only joy
Will come from living in hell

I know you're lost in the dark
But not by choice
Nonetheless in that darkness
you found your voice

And now here you are
A blessing in disguise
I know there's still light
Where darkness resides

As you float all alone
Dying in your blood bath
Wanting to end it all
Because some idiots laughed

Or for you to be so down
And so full of grief
That you pop pills and drop your chin
Into your chest and slowly
die in your sleep

From suicidal thoughts
that you thought were gone
But at last it's too late
And you sing your swan song.

SWAN SONG.

Silly Azz Love Poem

Love is like Coal
I'm gonna hold it till it's a diamond
Treat her like Everest
and then start climbing

Until I'm somewhere
Over the rainbow
And keep my fingers crossed
That she isn't a psycho

Hold her so tight
Till her lungs claps
Will she fall out of love for that
Maybe perhaps

But I'm so addicted 2U
So please don't get it twisted
That when I place my lips on top yours
I'm so uplifted

Nonetheless what else can I say
Except that you turn me on
That is why I had to write you
This silly azz love poem

SILLY AZZ LOVE POEM

Always Here

When I wake up in the morning
Someone is always here
When I go to sleep at night
Someone is always here
Hell even at high noon
Someone is always here
Somebody get this
Son of a bitch
A job application
So he can move the f@#k out of here.

The Wind Blows

Funny how your mind & mood
Changes like the wind blows
Before I could even blink good
It was off with your clothes

Or in the back seat of my jeep
Fogging up the windows
bouncing up & down
In tune with the tempo

And When you climax
It's like Niagara falls
But lust like this
Always Comes with pitfalls

The anticipation
of love making again
If I'm in too deep
Then I know I can't win

So I try to Play it cool
And Act like I've been there
But after months of playing house
I'm aware that Something's unclear

Because I tried to reach out
Then it started to snow
There was no response
And that's when the cold wind blows

I guess she changed her mind

THE WIND BLOWS

The Scale

For every Man or woman
There is a scale
That will determine in our lives
If we succeed or if we fail

On each side of that scale
There is good & evil
Trait's that infiltrate
And defines all people

Which way the scale will tilt
Nobody really knows
But sooner or later
Our destiny will show

The path that we will walk
For the rest of our lives
The good book also implies
That the eyes never lie

So come to grips with the fact
That we're one or the other
Some use blankets for tucking in
And others use to smother

So if there is good in your heart
You know which way to make the scale tilt
Or forever live in darkness
And tilt toward your guilt.

THE SCALE

Where Ever God Sends Her

The only thing I've ever loved
Just died in my arms
I held her dead body next to mine
Trying to keep her warm

She was my everything
The air that I breathe
With out her I am nothing
That's why I can't leave

I shake my fist to the sky
Asking God why
the only woman that I've ever loved is gone
And now I want to die

I feel so empty
Cold and abandoned
I wish my heart would just stop
And save me from this sadness

What have I done
Oh Lord have mercy
Ill repent my sinful ways
But please don't curse me

For to live without her
Is to not live at all
I know you can hear me
Since this is my down fall

I kiss my dead girl on the lips
and then I surrender
To join my beloved
Where ever God sends her.

WHERE EVER GOD SENDS HER.

Integrity

Please let me keep my integrity
Mirror, mirror, on the wall
Forever more in this life
And don't let me fall

Let me keep the qualities of being honest
A righteous man if I can
Who will fight the good fight
In this immoral and hostile land

In many ways my principles Are all I really have
That will not be compromised
No matter who or what Is standing in my path
I refuse to apologize

Because when the shit hits the fan
I will suffer with pride
I'll stand front and center of the storm
And I will take it with stride

My honor is everything
Admiration and respect
When it's all said and done
Our time with our family
Is all that we'll reflect

But no matter how strong the wind blows
No matter where my heartache is at
I will walk away unscathed
With my Integrity intact.

INTEGRITY

The Padawan & The Chosen one

Unwavering was her faith
To not give into hate
But to save her beloved master
It seems that it was too late

He was consumed by a darkness
His light died like a rose
When he lost the love of his life
His heart inside froze

Until he has become the one thing
That he one day swore to destroy
The boy who was once a slave
Will never again know joy

Just the pain of his survival
That burns like his defeat
At the hands of his former master
Revenge that's bittersweet

Will forever be a craving
Like a monster's stomach growls
Who is beneath the mask
Voices Whisper like an owl

As the war across the stars
Continues to violently rage
The dark side of the force
Has written a new page

And as a young Padawan girl
Realizes this revolution
She foresee s what is to come
The Death and devastation

From the single greatest person
She has ever known in her life

Has went and done the unthinkable
And has stepped away from the light

And as she recollects about her life
at the temple that was attacked and burned
Ashoka Tano finally realizes
That she must unlearn what she has learned

As she makes her way across the stars
And becomes Part of the myth
Of the chosen one who would bring balance
By ultimately becoming a Sith.

THE PADAWAN & THE CHOSEN ONE

Break My Heart

What lies beneath
Shallow feelings and contempt
What was once hard as steel
You have effortlessly bent

For your disrespect has no limits
But my love has depths
And the deep affection that once was
Has taught me too never hold my breath

And so I say to you my love
My heart is blue but forever true
Unknowing that love could ever hurt me
until I loved you

Besides the only thing remaining
Will be the memories of a glorious start
And how easy it was for you
To break my f*cking heart .

Cupid Can't Wait

I can still taste the sweet nectar of an old fling
that's bitter yet still sweet
This lingering desire like a vampire
Means that your cuisine I can't wait to eat

So I wait and anticipate
For glory days to once again become new
Unfortunately I'm not alone
And cupid says that "I can't wait to eat her too"

CUPID CAN'T WAIT.

The Combination

3 sons and a daughter
The perfect combination
Tumbling through my
Life 4 dates of celebration

1.
DAMIONTE
February 4th, my first child is born
To conquer and enlighten
So be forewarned

That my son Damionte's voice will be heard
When the Music plays
And universally accepted By fans
That's what the God's say

So good fortune in your past life
Right now, or Soon
And let the whole planet
Know it by writing It on the moon

Because your time will soon come
I can feel it in my heart
I always knew that you would shine DD Slim
And I knew this right from the start

So live out your dreams
And pick up the mic
Because when you let your dreams die son
You always die twice

2.
ROBERT
On December 19th a
beautiful bouncing boy
May every day be as sweet as a
Box of chips Ahoy

But the truth is Robert every day is a challenge
So you have to be a boss

And take full advantage
No matter the cost

And then you'll have the lady of your dreams
So say's the Greek God Eros
Or young jezebel queens feeding you grapes
Just Like the Egyptian pharaohs

But whatever it is you crave
Or whatever it is you desire
Never have limits
Keep reaching higher & higher

Because youth is not forever
Every day is a new page
Your gonna look up one day
And realize that you're your dads age

3.
JOSEPH
September 10th, once again
I'm blessed by providence
You're in the army now
To exert your dominance

Just know baby boy
And I say this loud
Corporal Joseph Owens
You make your old man proud

So love, rule, and conquer
that's what kings do
And only make decisions
From your heart and your mind
That continue to deem true

So peace in the middle east
Or wherever you are
And always wish big
In the presence of shooting stars

And any spoils of war
In this life you deserve it

You're the latest and greatest
And just know that you're worth it

4.
CATHERINE
December 10th the heavens
Sent me an angel
Beautiful inside and out
Perfection from every angle

Your mother raised you right
I'm eternally grateful
And if the love is still there
I will forever be thankful

For you're my only daughter
Crown jewel of my heart
Always & forever
Until from this world I must depart

So Catherine Alexa Owens
Princess, my baby girl
You are the last combination
To everything that I hold dear
In this cruel world

So remember you're my heart
Your love is everything
Even though we both know
Life is not always what it seems

So keep your head up
Because sometimes we all fall
And please rest assure
That I love you all

This was the combination to my
Heart, soul, mind & spirit
I just needed to convey this massage
One time so you kids would hear it......

Cupid's Blunder

Lovers became enemies
Enemies became friends
Cupid commits suicide
Because of this relationship that doesn't end

Strange how love happens
Even stranger how love can take you under
But I guess even the God's are baffled
By Cupid's blunder & wonder.

Cupid's Blunder

A Mother's Love

A mother's love transcends
From the beginning to the end
To always be victorious
And to walk away with the win

As she holds her baby close 2 heart
And snug in her arms
Mother's will meet death
Before baby comes to harm

Nothing is more moving
Than this unbreakable bond
A love so magical
It like it came from the tip of a magic wand

Everyone should be so lucky
To experience a love like this
But so many like myself
Doesn't know, that it exist..

A MOTHER'S LOVE

Eazy -E

Let's all have a moment of silence
For the soul reason the West Coast is on the map
And that reason is Eric wright
The God father of gangster rap

Your contributions will never be forgotten
So many owe you their career s
No matter how much time goes by
We will always remember the days of yesteryear

From Boyz in the hood
2 Coming straight out of Compton
You took the music industry by storm
And kept on stomping

Until you are now and forever
A Part of the culture
Who's style, swag, and image
Was fed on by a bunch of hip-hop vouchers

But you were a West Coast original
Who should have been crowned King
Str8 off the streets of Compton
Where 9mm sing

But be that as it may
You have inspired so many women and men
Your gospel will never be forgotten
Every time we turn to Eazy' s chapter 8 verse 10

Dedicated 2 a
West Coast original
Gangster Gangster

EAZY -E

THE BURNING KINGDOM OF BRIMSTONE

The Burning Kingdom of Brimstone Part 1

Enemies are everywhere
But I can't see the whites of their eyes
I don't kill because I'm brave
I do it to stay alive

Right now, it's fight or flight
So I choose to fight
Knowing the odds are on my side
Once we lose day light

All I hear is gun fire
And the shattering of glass
Voices outside the castle walls
Screaming for the soldiers to blast

But my walls are fortified
My defenses are impregnable
If I survive to see another sun
That would be delectable

But smoke is in the air
I can feel the flames
And the motivation of the
Killers who only want fame

So they can put me on display
Like Benito Mussolini
And embellish stories about the last time
That someone has seen me

But that day will never come
Because the sunset is done
As I quietly escape
Through my burning kingdom.

THE BURNING KINGDOM OF BRIMSTONE Part 1

The Burning Kingdom of Brimstone Part 2

Day light has turned into night
As citizens from my kingdom run away in fright
I disappear into the masses
Of poor and middle classes
And make my way north surrounded by assassin's

My kingdom for a day
Has had no reason to pray
But the siege on my castle
Will make my followers sway

With blood on my hands
And screaming for miles
I see dead body's stacked up
And burned in a pile

No man woman or child
Seems to be exempt
From This cruelty of evil
That I never would have dreamt

So with My blade in hand
I attack from the shadows
As I make my way swiftly and quickly
To Princess Catherine of Alexa by noon tomorrow

For peace is no more
The country is in a blaze
Anyone who survives
No doubt will be slaves

So when I arrive
I shall Mastermind a plan
That will crush my enemies completely
In these fair lands.

BURNING KINGDOM OF BRIMSTONE
part 2

The Burning Kingdom of Brimstone Part 3

I've traveled many miles
with a few more to go
Collecting all of my thoughts
So that my plan will flow

My daughter rule's Alexa
That has a treaty with Tahiti
Who uses chemical war fair
To annihilate city's

But she will never agree
She now rules with compassion
And then I'll be forced to hear
All about her dissatisfactions

But I am still her father
And I am still King
Yet family ties have been a problem
Since I've buried my queen

That's when my daughter
Became cold and distant
And refuse to listen
Much to my dismay no matter how persistent

Yet time will surely tell
If it's all water under the bridge
Or if forgiveness is off the table
For all the wrong that I did

But enough reminiscing I'm at
Princess Catherine's castle doors
And now it's finally time for me
Plant the seeds of war....

THE BURNING KINGDOM of BRIMSTONE Part 3

The Burning Kingdom of Brimstone Part 4

Standing at the draw bridge
I got the strangest feeling
What do I do if my daughter
isn't ready & willing

The draw bridge finally drops
and I slowly enter
As I exhale I see my breath
because of the cold of winter

I begin to look up and marvel
At a familiar face
that quickly runs down the stairs
with open arms and a warm embrace

Then with tears in her eyes
She begins to sigh
And without saying a word
I knew that to many years had gone by

But time heals all wounds
That fact I can't deny
We only have two choices in this life
And that is to live or to die

Yet even as I relished in this moment
Of Love & understanding
I still know time is of the essence
And I have to start planning

Now that old wounds have healed
And I'm finally restored
The time has finally come
To unequivocally take these Son of a bitches to war.

THE BURNING KINGDOM OF BRIMSTONE Part 4

The Burning Kingdom of Brimstone Part 5

My daughter Catherine of Alexa
supplied me everything that I need
To Maine and destroy
And to make my enemies bleed

Thousands of loyal troops
Are ready to march in their boots
Many soldiers will die
Is the only absolute

But I shall fear no death
As I stump through this valley
playing little Richard's
long tall Sally

But I anticipate the worst
My heart starts to hurt
Plus if I want to survive
I have to stay alert

As we are getting ever so closer
Some of my soldiers start to pray
Intuitive enough to know
That today is the day

We're only 2 klicks away
Before we take back what's ours
Before we step over the enemies body
Or the enemy steps over ours

So everybody lock and load
It's time to take some souls
Because we're about to walk the walk
Of Along bloody road.

THE BURNING KINGDOM OF BRIMSTONE Part 5

The Burning Kingdom of Brimstone Part 6

I've got murder on my mind
But I must think clearly
And command from the front
So that my soldiers will hear me

Napoleon Bonaparte said that
" The battlefield is a scene of constant chaos
And the winner will be the one
who controls that chaos "

So I must organize the confusion and shoot to kill
I give a f@#k
How the international committee
of war crimes feels

My people will be liberated
Me and my soldiers vindicated
Soon after the scum of this earth
Has been annihilated

It's been said that our heavenly father
kills indiscriminately
And when it comes to dealing with these animals
So shall we

Off with their head's
Fill their bodies full of lead
Evil dies tonight
will be the only history that's read

And reparations for the victims
after all that they've been through
but what else would you expect
if the oppressed
Had been you

But the history of the world
has always been to destroy and rebuild
And to make something of this life
for our loved ones that have tragically been killed

So let us not forget
The pain and sacrifice
Of all the men and women of this war
Who have paid the ultimate price

Because when war is on the rise
That's when liberty dies

And we will quickly be reminded
As we stare into dead eyes

That's why we never stop fighting
For love or for freedom
Because as long as there's tomorrow
We can rebuild our burning kingdom.

THE BURNING KINGDOM OF BRIMSTONE Part 6
THE END.

SAD CLOWN

Sad Clown Part 1

Smiling behind my tears
makes my heart hurt
Being angry all the time
is too much work

Laughing for no reason
is just annoying
I'm so f@#king out of my mind
I don't know what I'm enjoying

But most clowns are sad
when they get knocked down
That's why my frowns upside down
When you start to drown

I feel some kind of joy
Watching you gasping for air
Instead of lending you a hand
I reach for a chair

And watch you go under
As you're calling for Christ
But I remember all of the times
that you laughed at this clown's life

So now I can laugh
At you splashing around
As I'm having visions and thoughts
Of the last time I got knocked down

Now I must bid you goodbye
Without a moment to spare
Because now this sad clown
Can enjoy the day, and the fresh air .

SAD CLOWN. Part 1

Sad clown Part 2

I have big clown feet
Red hair and a nose
A smile to die for
Wearing baggy ass clothes

I always light up
When the sun goes down
Because my empathy for human life
Starts to shutdown

I'll do a dumb dance
And then slip on a banana pill
Just to pay the rent
Humiliation kills

All I hear is people chuckling
And laughing at my pain
Once you've tasted the tear drops of a clown
You'll never be the same

So don't you ever make the mistake
Of getting to close to my tent
The last kid that kicked me in the ass disappeared
And hasn't been seen again since

So show some respect
Next time you're in a strange town
And be careful not to slip
On the tear drops
of a sad clown.

SAD CLOWN Part 2

Sad Clown Part 3

Standing in the mirror
Applying my clown paint
What I feel in my heart
Is far from a saint

I don't have anything
No wife, no kids
Just the alcohol that's on my breath
And the tears that are forming underneath my eyelids

I feel so ashamed sometimes
About my occupation
Being the object of ridicule
All across this nation

But what can I do
It's Part of my prison work release program
Either I go out here and make a fool of myself
Or it's back in the can

So I put on my wig
And my big red clown nose
My outfit with the polka dots
That I put on over my street clothes

I'm so f@#king nervous
That I close my eyes and count to 7
And pick up the candy that I dropped on the floor
And then I kiss it up to heaven

Now it's all most show time, So all of you
kids and weekend parents gather around
Because you're about to be entertained
by the tears of a clown.

SAD CLOWN Part 3

Sad Clown Part 4

My coworker fat Joey
Was walking on a tight rope
The crowd began to applaud
As a sign of hope

For a 400 pound daredevil
Defying the odds while eating cake
If he slips and falls
It's gonna sound like an earthquake

So I stand around with the crowd
Doing my juggling act
With so many in attendance
I know most of the fans will surely come back

But fat Joey miss steps
And begins to struggle
He falls to his death
As I continued to juggle

So I walk over to fat Joey
And look right in his face
Just to wonder why he didn't notice
That I had untied his shoe lace

The crowd continues to scream
And runs away from the circus in a panic
Now that fat Joey is gone
I can work on my magic

And become the main attraction
Yeah I like how that sounds
Fat Joey would be proud
Too bad he's not around.

SAD CLOWN Part 4

Sad Clown Part 5

How can this be, every day I walk around
Kicking my heels in the air
While I'm dying inside
With this image like I just don't care

So I continue to live a lie
Till I start to regurgitate
Everything that makes me sad
And everything that I hate

Like making other people laugh
At my own expense
But I guess being a clown
Lacks any kind of common sense

I'm no Krusty the clown
pennywise, Or Homie
I'm just a pathetic sad clown
Who is always lonely

That's why when I see a happy couple
At my show and they start to kiss
I hit them in the face with a cream pie
That's full of horse shit

And before they can comprehend
exactly what happened
I disappear into crowd
While the audience is laughing

Devious I am indeed
Diabolical in my ways
If I truly had my way
You'd be digging your own grave

So please before you judge me
And try to bring me down
Just remember who I am
A pathetic sad face Clown.

SAD CLOWN Part 5

Sad Clown Part 6

There's this prick of a kid named Andy
Who always kicks me in my shins
When I'm on my smoke break
Now let the plotting begin

I Dance over to this prick
And grab him by the ear
Pull him behind the circus tent
And feel his heart full of fear

Then I proceed to let him know
That this is it
For the last 3 times that he kicked me
And made me drop my cigarettes

Kid You're about to get this
Size 16 clown shoe
Because I'm gonna be kicking your little ass
Until I'm smelling dodo

Then I caught myself
Am I really this foul
Probably explains why it hurts
Every time that I smile

But if I don't go through with it
This little prick will be back at it soon
So I proceeded to cock my foot back
And kicked his little ass to the moon

And maybe that will teach
This little prick a valuable lesson
Just because someone's a clown
Doesn't mean that they're the ones to be testing.

SAD CLOWN Part 6

Sad Clown Part 7

Love is in the air
I can smell the flowers
But I can also smell me
Damn I need a shower

So I can wash this paint off my face
And put it on again
What a way to make a living
This paint is f@#king with my skin

But I ain't nothing to look at
So it doesn't even matter
With the kind of luck that I've had
It's like a mirror has shattered

But now I'm shit out of luck
Stuck in a rut
The next happy S.O.B That smiles at me
Is getting f@#ked up

But even if he runs
I'll still be a step behind
And because of my PTSD
His ass will be mine

because I'm vindictive
and for no f@#king reason
That's why 7 days a week for me
Is the killing season

But I'm starting to get tired
Of giving into my hate
For me there was never any choice
That's why it's too late

So when I jump into the back
Of your Uber or Lyft
The last sound that you will hear
Will be when the gear shifts.

SAD CLOWN Part 7

Sad Clown Part,8

I can't take it no more
The voices in my head
Are they people that I've killed
Wishing that I was dead

But how much more dead could I be
I'm alive but I'm soulless
I Paint my face to hide the hate
To conceal that I'm hopeless

I try to blend in
and bring some kind of joy
Funny how the same levity I bring
I somehow destroy

I miss fat Joey
But he was steeling my shine
Every laugh and applause In this circus
Could and should be rightfully mine

Or maybe it's just me
I'm just a sad face clown
Who can make all of noise in the world
And still not make a sound

So for now I'll crack these eggs on your head
And blind you with the egg yolk
And boot you in your ass with a knife
Which Is one of my sickest jokes

But you just wait
For what I got hidden underneath my pajamas
The sight of everyone running for their lives
Is gonna be bananas.

SAD CLOWN Part 8

Sad clown Part 9

The greatest show on earth
Giggling and cotton candy
Little people in abundance
And a fortune teller named Mandy

Who swears she can see the future
with her psychic abilities
Who wants to earn enough money
For her peace of mind and tranquility

She's the apple of my eye
But she doesn't know I exist
I pulled a rabbit out of my hat
And she told me that, "I have to take a piss"

I performed my best magic
And barley got a laugh
She behaved really unladylike
And started digging in her ass

Then she breaks out her crystal ball
Pulls it to her lips and gives it a kiss
And says "I can scene a deep sadness
With imminent danger and a risk"

Now she's really turning me off
So I show her my knife trick
I put an apple on her head
And then I intentionally miss

Because if she was really f@#king psychic
And Mandy was so got damn profound
She would have known the end result
For f@#king with a sad clown.

SAD CLOWN Part 9

Sad Clown Part 10

I think my time is up
My time as a clown
How can I be happy
When so much tragedy is around

Fat men falling off of tight ropes
People being gutted in circus tents
Arrogant bastards drowning nearby
And juvenile delinquents being shot off the fence

I just can't take it no more
Every few weeks a new town
A chance to make the innocent laugh
And for those who get on my nerves
To be taken down

But who am I kidding
After prison this is all that I know
Bringing joy to people lives
And f@#king people up that don't like the show

So maybe I'll hang around
Just a little bit longer
Smoke a pack of cigarettes a day
To see if my lungs get any stronger

And deal with the hand
That I've been dealt
And make you feel things
That you've never felt

So here I come world
I hope you're ready for me
Because after I make you laugh
I'm gonna make you feel
This clowns misery

With a little hocus pocus
And some abracadabra
I'm about to make you disappear
Right after I stab ya.

The End

SAD CLOWN Part 10

I Still Love You So

I still love you so
And I can't let go
Why we ever parted ways
I guess I'll never know

But if you ever come back to me
Likes Halley's comet
I swear to love you more
Than the way that you wanted

But what can I say
Except for, life is for learning
And I will love you always
As this world is turning

Now let me whisper in your ear
Something that I think you'll want to know
After all of these years
I still love you so.

I STILL LOVE YOU SO.

D.e.r.e.o.n

Delightfully charming and full of personality
Every day is a risky step and I wish you longevity
Raised you from a child, years I won't forget
Early to bed and early to rise please don't forget
Oceans run deep but not as deep as my memories
Never forget my love for you and always remember me

Sail around the world, see all that you can see
Court beautiful women be all that you can be
Once I found love but it tore me apart
To teach you must learn so protect your mind & your heart
To be or not to be remains to be the question in this world full of lies & truths of broken lessons.

DEREON SCOTT

UFOs Or Drones

Strange sightings in the sky
The media & government says that it's drones
But what if they're all wrong
And we're not alone

In this infinite galaxy
That we call the milky way
Will this spark a celebration
Or motivate many to pray

About extraterrestrial beings
And their true intentions
With the hierarchy of this world
When their greeted with condescension

Cries & Lies

Vigilante justice is in the air
Health care issues are at a feverish pitch
What makes another human beings' life less than
Simply because they're not rich

The haves need to do some soul searching
The have nots need a health plan
How many more people need to die
Before the right side takes a stand

Because we can no longer delay
And you can no longer deny
But to depose of those who selfishly use their power
Might be the solution to all of the cries and lies.

Key 2 Righteousness

We weren't meant to be humble
We were meant to be humbled
No matter your status in this life
Sooner or later castle's do crumble

It doesn't matter if you're rich
Or known worldwide
There are things that will bring you to your knees
That will make the most cold-blooded of us cry

Because beauty does fade
As does money that we've made
True believers are a minority
Amongst those who will be saved

So when you ask what's on the other side
Best believe it's only what you take with you
The good deeds and memories of those you've touched
Will be the key 2 righteousness to see things through

KEY 2 RIGHTEOUSNESS

Choose

Should I give up on life
Or should I continue fight
I'm torn between dying in the dark
Or living in the light

Do I Lean toward righteousness
Or do I self-destruct
Live by society's rules
Or live my life like I just don't give a f@#k

The most dangerous human being in this world
Is the one with nothing to lose
And sooner or later there will come a time
When we will all have to choose

CHOOSE.

kindness Is A Curse

The more I interact with people
The more I realize that I don't fit in
I've been cursed 2 be a kind soul by nature
And it's because of this, that I will never win

Unless I sacrifice my freedom, life and position
That's next to the father
And turn and burn pages from the Bible
and unapologetically spit on the author's

For making me believe that if I have faith
then my life won't get any worse
But the sad truth of it all is that
kindness is a curse

KINDNESS IS A CURSE.

Boss Lady

Boss lady of all boss ladies
always beautiful and elegant
A vision of pure class
With a nice round ass

I love your brown skin
The way you always win
I love your style of fashion
From beginning to end

Dominant on the clock
But I can sense a pinch of shyness
When I'm in your presence
I always want to say "your highness "

I don't have a crush
Or butterflies like when someone's enchanted
I just have a ton of respect
That makes me feel romantic

For the lady boss of all bosses
Who deserves a thrown
A benevolent ruler of your kingdom
Is all you've ever shown

But in another time
I would have made you mine
And I mean this sincerely
It's not just a line

So may every day of your life
Be a celebration
And I will crown you personally
At your next inauguration.

Boss Lady......

Bob Marley

Beautiful and so different
That rastafari sound
That took you around the world
With dreadlocks underneath your crown

You moved mountains with your words
Exodus made you a star
You are the undisputed king of reggae
And that title is yours by far

One love was such an inspiration
No one could have done it better
You unified Jamaica peacefully
So that everyone could come together

So I tilt my hat to you King
Bob Marley I truly love you brother
You left your mark on this cruel world
And you did it like no other.

((((((BOB MARLEY))))))))))

A Hard Farewell

Isn't it something how evil Can swoop down
and cause havoc in your life
Disrupting everything so easily
In the day or the night

I wonder why nothing good
Ever happens just as easy
If my life is cut down too soon
Would it be because God needs me

To be up there with him
More than I need to be down here in this hell
But as difficult as this life has been
It will still be hard to say farewell.

A HARD FAREWELL

Childhood Missed

Children grow up so fast
Sometimes faster than you can think
All of those precious moments
Gone in an eye blink

My son's coming of age
My daughter becoming a butterfly
An incomplete canvas of memories
That will remain unfinished until I die

Funny how the things we want most
We're destined to never have
Even now as I'm writing this
I can hear the God's laugh

At a tormented soul
Who lived his life in a bottomless pit
That tried to hold on to his Children's childhood
Only just to miss it.

Childhood Missed

A Beautiful Darkness

There is a beautiful darkness
In the eyes of the king
Who lived a good life
And has everything

But everything that he has
Comes with a cost
His triumph can only be measured
By how much he's lost

The love of his children
Has been replaced with sacrifice
For absolute power
And a heart that is cold as ice

And even though love is nonexistent
To a king that has been perceived as charmless
If you look into his eyes
You can still see a beautiful darkness.

Trip 2 Hell

My mind is spinning
Everything is a blur
God only knows
What's about to occur

I can hear screaming in my ears
And a mist of tears
Also the bad energy
Of a strange one's fears

I'm feeling light headed
Anxious and even high
If this is a trip to hell
I pray we don't fry

So God if you can hear me
I swear to you, no more lies
That's when we finally slowed down and stopped
On the tea cup ride.

Coming home from war

The warrior is gone
And left all alone
With nothing more to give
Except for these bear bones

And the trauma of a time
When most of my friends died
But now that the war is finally over
All I want to do is just hide

From the world and myself
Because All I know is killing
Uncle Sam turned me into a monster
And now expects for me to be a civilian

But I don't know if I can do it
Lord knows I'm gonna try
But if I don't succeed
It's because I already died.

Damsel

If you're familiar with the city of love
then you know Mademoiselle lives in France
But she would very much like to marry
an American man

So she flies to Hollywood
In the city of Angels
And meets a fast talking low life
Who was wearing a kangol

And he sells her a dream
About being a star
Finding true love
And driving fancy cars

All you've got to do
Is stay close to me
And of course Mademoiselle
Replied with oui

But unbeknown to this young lady
Things were about to go awry
As his true colors would soon show
As she looks into his eyes

He said his name was pookie
And you're about to sell what's under that dress
That's when Mademoiselle from France
Became a damsel in destress

Love Makes You Feel

Love makes you feel weak
Love makes you feel strong
Love makes you feel like
You always belong
Love makes you feel appreciated
Love makes you feel safe
Love is always on time
Because love won't wait
Love makes you feel important
Love always listens
Love will always remind you
When it goes missing
Love makes you feel secure
Love never makes you feel poor
Because there is no hell
That love can't endure
Love makes you feel tender
Sometimes love has a past
But when that love is true
Love holds till the last.

Calm before the Storm

The calm before the storm
A gentle breeze & falling leaves
Nothing to indicate
That you should indeed take heed

Nothing that tells you
To respect the silence
Because every hurricane
Slowly builds up into violence

And after it arrives
All you can do is weather the storm
Some people are like this
Since the day they were born

So be mindful of disrespecting someone
And expecting the norm
Because the other person's silence
Is usually the calm before the storm

You Can Lose

You can lose in life
You can lose in love
You can lose all of the blessings
That come from above

You can lose your family
You can lose your dreams
I know it's hard to comprehend
As hard as it seems

You can lose everything
Till you say enough is enough
But don't ever lose
Because you gave up

Before

I want to go back
And do everything in reverse
Before I thought of my life
As this terrible curse

Decade after decade
Back to my youth
If I truly had a choice
I'd go back as far as my first tooth

Before the insecurities
Before I knew what it is to be loveless
Before my first steps
Before I knew what it is to be hug less

Or maybe as far back
As the day that my parents met
So they can never meet
And save me from a life
That I could never except

Life Can Still Amaze

What do we have in common
Love, Life, fantasies and stars
The stories of my life
Have now become ours

The joys of living
And the agony of defeat
Conquest that made me proud
And dreams I'll never reach

And love that I mistakenly
Thought was my birth right
Would never come to fruition
No matter how hard I would fight

But be that as it may
Love has left me scared
By a pain that was ordained
And written in the stars

So may God bless all of the eyes
That gaze upon this page
And remember no matter how sad life can get
As long as we keep living, life can still amaze.

Life can still amaze.

Find What You are looking for

Peace is something that we all search for
But few of us seldom find
Not in the physical sense
Nor in the mind

But I wish you all good prudence
As you embark on this journey
And find what it is you're looking for
But only if you are worthy.

FIND WHAT YOU ARE LOOKING FOR.

Paradise Lost

When Paradise is lost
It's forever lost
And nothing can return it
No matter the cost

The innocents of a child
Will vanish with their smile
And perhaps will come to be
Oh too familiar with exile

So listen to your children
Even when they don't speak
I was a victim as a child
And it didn't plague me for weeks

It didn't plague me for months
It plagued me for years
And it doesn't go away
It doesn't disappear

And sure there are times
When you're not so nervous
But the experience is still there
Right below the surface

Furthermore I tell you this
So another child doesn't pay the cost
And becomes the next boy or girl
To have their paradise lost

PARADISE LOST

Who Am I

Who am I
I don't really know
I would give anything
for the truth to show

Life without living
Is a terrible thing
It's like your vocal cords are cut
With this longing to sing

Constantly moving
with no destination
And stifled in this life
From my poor education

Love I've never felt
That dream is no more
I guess I'm someone
Whom love has no allure

Wars have been fought
For love and for honor
But the more that I ponder
I realize that I'm a monster

That tries to fit in
With my mask of sanity
Till someone realizes
My Shakespearean tragedy

And knows that I'm beyond
Any normal comprehension
As being in my presence
Breeds some kind of tension

So please let me be
In my fortress of solitude
And avoid the unpleasantness
Of hostile attitudes

And maybe someday
Hopefully before I die
There will be an answer
To who the hell am I.

WHO AM I?

Learning 2 Flourish

Learning to flourish
Starts with courage
Decisions that we make
Will have to be worth it

Because if you deserve it
The universe will serve it
And then all good things
Will come to the surface

Learning to flourish
Is like wings and flight
And you'll need to be ambitious
To reach new heights

But please keep in mind
That flourishing never stops
It can be a cold & desolate place
Because it's very lonely at the top.

LEARNING 2 FLOURISH

Eternity Begins

I don't feel anything anymore
Anger, happiness, or pain
Just this empty Shell of a man
Is all that remains

My youth use to be
so damn adventurous
Cohabitating with other predators
that were so damn treacherous

Surviving the street life
Morning, noon and night
But something inside my life
is not quite right

Lady luck skipped town
Along time ago
Without even saying goodbye
But then again she never said hello

Time is running out
Time is running thin
At the end of it all
Is where eternity begins.

ETERNITY BEGINS

The Fractured Lights

Spellbinding magnificent lights
Beam through the dark night
Blinding all of the occupants
That gaze up at the sight

Surrounded by the four elements
Earth, wind, fire, and water
Moses saw the same thing
Right before a biblical Slaughter

But life comes and goes
Like the beginning and end
And the fractured light is just a beacon
To where we're all going, and to where we've all been

But such things are formalities
That have been written in the stars
And if you read between the lines
You will see God's memoirs

He said that the earth shall be done
As it is in heaven
But only after the 7 signs of revelations
Have all come together

So embrace the fractured light
Because it comes with love
But you should also beware
Of the fury from above

So please, come as you are
Just like a thief in the night
For you are about to be judged
Beneath and underneath
the fracturing of lights.

THE FRACTURED LIGHTS

Love's Only Value Exist

A real lady always makes love
Feel exciting and new
And makes a man feel like
There's nothing he wouldn't do

Rob, steel, or kill
Just to stay in favor
And lay down his own life
When it's time to save her

Nothing is 2 far
And nothing is 2 near
But the Tweety Birds around my head
Keeps me from seeing clear

Because the only thing in my focus
Is god's gift to man
And I knew that gift was a woman
From just a mere glance

Beautiful, soft, feminine,
And not to mention eloquent
The mountains I'll have to climb
For real love is irrelevant

There's nothing a man won't suffer
No sea he won't swim
Even if his chances are looking bleak
and his future is looking grim

Because Love's Only Value Exist
When you persist
to rock your girlfriend to sleep
and leave her with a goodnight kiss

So never drift away
And be back before it's dawn
On the eve of the storm
to hold her in your arms

Because Loves Only value Exist
When you persist
To let the one's you love know
That when they are gone, they will be missed.

LOVES ONLY VALUE EXIST

Let Me Down Easy

I love to play hard
and love even harder
If she loves me back
I'll never disregard her

I love the sound of children
gleeful and laughing
While the waves on the beach
are constantly crashing

I want a beautiful woman
that's rocking my T-shirt
That knows what it is
when I ask for dessert

And serve me like a waitress
Like it doesn't even matter
Oh my how I love
Hot sex on a platter

Or the formalities of loyalty
When someone kisses my ring
A relaxed state of mind
That only Sade Adu can bring

I love to be loved
Even though it sounds cheesy
So if you decide to let me down
Then let me down easy.

LET ME DOWN EASY.

The Question Is?

What is a king
With out a kingdom
Tell me what are people
If they don't have freedom

You Tell the one you love
It's love, but you beat them
You tell them they can leave
But you never release them

Tell me what is happiness
When you're Drowning in tears
You tell me that you're safe
But you're so full of fear

Tell me, why do people
That smile In your face
Are so full of envy
That it's borderlines with hate

And tell me why do you rejoice
When you're so full of sorrow
Tell me what is today
If there's no tomorrow

And tell me why we put our faith
in something we can't see
But when it's right in our face
We just can't believe

And why do we have to die
Before we get what we're worth
When our heaven and our hell
Is right here On this earth

Why is the question
Why is the debate
I hope we find the answer soon
Before it's too late
Why.

THE QUESTION IS?

The Juice is Free

Cold blooded killer
Or misunderstood
Should he be remembered as number 32
Or the murders in Brentwood

For rushing 2003 yards
Or running from the police
For being hated for not being locked up
Or loved for his release

Who was just a poor street kid
That dared to dream
And would one day be blessed
To have a dream team

But none that matters
Not anymore
Because OJ Simpson
Will no longer score

Gone from this world
But not from our memories
A star athlete
Immortalized in infamy

So don't squeeze the juice
For only God can judge
Orenthal James Simpson
Of all of his sins that was

Hence love him or hate him
OJ is finally free
A man who was acquitted
But never really free.

THE JUICE IS FREE
07/09/1947
04/10/2024

Life Care

Life Care is taking care
Care for your life
Not the kind of care
That you have for an ex-wife

I'm talking about the kind of care
That was always there
Not in your early life
But in your mid life

Cause if your 18 and mean
And someone makes you flick your knife
Then it's all downhill
Because of a lowlife

When you could have had it all
The finer things in life
Not only living life
But living the highlife

So become pro-life
Care for your life
Before your sentenced to a term
That's longer than life

Because the really lucky ones
Become bigger than life
And if you're unlucky in this game
You become jack knifed

So avoid the street life and the wild life
Before life itself doesn't care
And you're in the afterlife
For living half a life that was still true to life
But live it like you want because it's your life.

LIFE CARE.

Love Is Like Wine

Love is like wine
But it depends on How much you can take
To sip it hurts nobody
But to empty the bottle is to invite a headache

How many times have we emptied the bottle
And overindulged in more than just drink
Drunk off of the passions of love
And drunk to the point where we can't think

And become lost in what appears to be
A tidal wave of lust and emotions
But sip the wine slowly my friends
Or fall victim to your devotions

You will stare into the eyes
Of the one that will make your heart sink
That will captivate you to the point
Where you will refuse to blink

Because you won't want to miss a thing
From the object of your affections
And when you're feeling fine from the wine
Nothing beats this connection

But when you empty the bottle
Love becomes unhinged
And you'll start hearing things like
"Where are you going", and "where the fuck have you been"

Moreover, you'll start to realize
That there's a thin line between love and hate
And it will ether make you very violent
Are so unhappy that you will start to shake

Furthermore, you'll start to reminisce
About How did we get here
When we were tipsy off each other's love
It was nothing but cheers

And then reality sets in
"Oh my God I'm in trouble"
As your lover raps their hands around your throat
And begins to throttle

Then with your dying last breath
Right before your limp body is toppled
You glance over to see a blood stained
Empty wine bottle

So everybody please remember
And please don't forget
That too sip the wine of love hurts nobody
But to empty the bottle is to invite a headache.

LOVE IS LIKE WINE

You Have 2 Live with Yourself

You got to live for yourself
Because you've got to live with yourself
You are unique in every way
Unlike anybody else

There will be things that are wrong for others
But they will be just right for you
Sometimes we have to ignore public opinions
And do what we've got to do

Life can be a scary place
There's no doubt about it
Everybody knows this to be true
There's no need to shout it

Just take a deep breath
And tell yourself today's the day
That I take my destiny into my own hands
No matter what the haters say

So don't be afraid
Because you've got to live for yourself
And don't do anything that you'll regret
Because you still have to live with yourself.

      YOU HAVE 2 LIVE WITH YOURSELF.

To Live for Nothing

I want a love that will stay
That would be nice
Someone I could confide in
For the rest of my life

When it's cold outside
And the sky is raging
A vision of loveliness
That keeps my heart racing

I've never had the pleasure
Of ecstasy and bliss
Or paralyzed from the emotions
From just one kiss

Because the second that I care
I know that She will be gone
Then love will cast me out
and leave me withdrawn

But what do I do
If I somehow fail
Love is unforgiving
If you don't prevail

Yet he who is not courageous
Accomplishes nothing
And to live without love
Is to live for nothing

TO LIVE FOR NOTHING

Reciprocated

This is why the word reciprocated
Is so sophisticated
Only those who truly know God
Will ever appreciate it

favor for a favor
In the eyes of your lover
Simply means that
One good turn deserves another

So you better live and learn
And don't let your soul burn
Forever is everlasting
Just be aware when it's your turn

That if we ever cross paths
somewhere in paradise
I'll make sure to let you know
that I'm glad you made it

And if I don't see you there
somewhere in paradise
I'll know It was because
When God showed you love
you never reciprocated

RECIPROCATED

The Inevitable

The inevitable soon will come
And when it comes, it will come for us all
I hope there's something else out there
Beyond the mist and the fog

Beyond the tears that I will carry
On my one-way trip to the grave
Old friends I will see there
And friends that I have not yet made

For the inevitable is frightening
But I won't let it make me a slave
This journey is something we all must go through
Rather you are a coward or brave

And once this masquerade is over
We will lie in the bed that we've made
And as our life passes us bye
So will the parade.

THE INEVITABLE

Queen of Today & Tomorrow

You're the alpha and omega
The beginning and end
No one has ever been more beautiful & elegant
And a shining example for women

A voice so angelic and Devine
That it can tame the savage beast
There's no one else like you
When I hear you all I can think about is peace

It's a war of the hearts
But warring hearts make you pray
That if I ever had you
I would truly cherish the day

And wait for the exact moment
When you would tell me that "your love is king"
In a diamond life paradise
Is where you would begin to sing

Then I would pull you by my side
On a moonlit dark night
As I stare into your eyes
And give you the kiss of life

So Helen Folasade Adu
just know that you can't hide
Because you already know that
Love is stronger than pride

And no more songs
About the king of sorrow
Because you're my Queen of today
And Queen of tomorrow.

You Left Me Too Soon

You keep selling me a dream
About how we're gonna be together
Against insurmountable odds
In any kind of weather

About how your love will be unshakable
And always be on time
Forsake all others that come around
As well as be exclusively mine

Yet you threaten to leave
Expecting for me to be mad
But the truth of the matter is dear
I never miss, what I never had

YOU LEFT ME 2 SOON.

The Pursuit of Happiness

The pursuit of happiness
Will I ever get it
It's so Anonymous and rare
And fades into the air

I'm always on its tail
But it always alludes me
Happiness is playing hard to get
I think it knows what it's doing to me

Making me wait
just until it's too late
Sounds mean spirited and cruel
When you've been waiting from out of the gate

To hit a home run, slam dunk
Scour a touchdown in this life
I wonder will I ever get through
all of the stress & strife

And you can miss with the golden years
I don't believe the hype
That life at the end
Is gonna be so dandy and nice

Living in a convalescent
Waiting to be the next contestant
On who will kick the bucket
what happened to adolescents

And doing it all over again
Like Benjamin button
And If I die as a baby
It won't be for nothing

Or maybe somehow
I can change unhappiness
And then I'll get another shot
At the pursuit of happiness.

THE PURSUIT OF HAPPINESS

Down the Line

I can't believe that you're gone
Oh how I wish you could have lived forever
But forever has come to pass
As I reminisce through the bottom of a shot glass

And I try to kill at will
the pain the blame and the shame
As I try to come to grips
With not seeing you again

MY memories of you are so vivid
Image's that I will cherish in my heart
For the end is now the beginning
And with God, you will have a fresh start

But fear not baby sister
Because everyone has their time
And I promise 2 see you again
Somewhere down the line.

DOWN THE LINE.
Dedicated 2 STACI GUYDON

What is Loneliness

What is it 2 be
Empty, abandoned, and hollow
To be trapped in the belly of the beast
Where loved ones will never follow

2 no longer be connected
Isolated and secluded
This feeling usually will creep
When the victims are clueless

Until at last it is to late
We're in the back of beyond
And the reason we were never found
Is because our loved ones are glad that we're gone

Loneliness will break your heart
Again and again
But it's better to be lonely
Than be surrounded by enemies
who are disguised as friends.

WHAT IS LONELINESS

Marvelous Marvin Gaye

How sweet it is
Too be loved by you
I heard it through the grapevine
I just hope that it isn't true

That we lost the greatest R&B singer
Too have ever touch our souls
When God made you
He truly broke the mold

You made us look at ourselves
And the world that we live in
What's going on
Would be when the journey begins

But then the unthinkable would happen
On April fool's day
It was 1984
But it feels like yesterday

That you would be gunned down
Marvelous Marvin Gaye
Would be forever silenced
By love that went astray

But you will never be forgotten
Your legacy will live on
Murdered by your dad
Just to die in your mom's arms.

MARVELOUS MARVIN GAYE

The Galveston Giant

Where did you come from
How were you so free
At a time in American history
When liberty was on her knees

No one dared to speak out
Yet there you were
The sports writers of that time
Had no idea what was about to occur

Fighting against a system
That was 60 years away from civil rights
With all of the death threats
I often wondered how did you make it through the night

You made love to women that were forbidden
That could have sealed your fate
The atmosphere you lived in
Was Dangerously toxic and so full of hate

You knocked your oppressors down
And then dared them to get up
Then you would smile with your gold teeth
And tell them to shut the hell up

You were such a brave soul
I wish I had that kind of bravery in me
To be that oppressed
But still live your life, like you were free

And to be a blinding light
To so many precious boys and girls
When you became the first black
Heavy weight champion of the world.

THE GALVESTON GIANT

Dedicated 2 Jack Johnson

Betrayal

I've been bamboozled a second time
Just like the first
Funny how the second time
Feels a little bit worse

I can see I'm unwanted
So I guess I won't stay
Traitors are not defined by themselves
But by who they betray

Now that I know for a fact
That it's just me, myself, and I
The monkey that was on my back
Just laid down and died

The same way that you will die
So brace yourself for a tragedy
Just because someone's born into your family
Doesn't mean that they're family

So take a long hard look
At the person you've become
And do some soul searching
While you're still young

Because if you don't
The good in your life will soon be derailed
And then you your self will feel the sting
Of a loved one's betrayal

BETRAYAL.

Cast Out For All 2 See

The fall of one of God's archangel's
Full of wisdom and perfect in beauty
Has been cast out of heaven
Because of his pride and unholy cruelty
Once anointed by the merciful
And shined so blindingly bright
But now makes mortal men take heed
By bewaring of the light
From the one that is now the father of lies
That held such a high position
I know there were feelings of sadden righteousness
When God made his final decision
And Jesus said, "oh how you have fallen from heaven
Morning star, son of the dawn"
His spirit brother was finally gone
Because of the treachery he had spawned
And now Lucifer is exiled and expelled
As the Almighty teaches him a valuable lesson
While Jesus and the rest of the angels intently watch
The prince of darkness fall like lightning from heaven.

The End

The end of everything
Is the beginning of all
Your Spirit slowly rises
As your eye lids fall

Too the coming of the Sun
After the dead of night
May you all find peace
At the end of your twilight

THE END.

www.ingramcontent.com/pod-product-compliance
Lightning Source LLC
LaVergne TN
LVHW021816060526
838201LV00058B/3410